Another Look
at
Bible Study

Another Look at Bible Study

The Misuse of II Timothy 2:15 and the Abuse of Christ's Body

Clyde L. Pilkington, Jr.

BIBLE STUDENT'S PRESS™

Windber, Pennsylvania

Another Look at Bible Study: The Misuse of II Timothy 2:15 and the Abuse of Christ's Body
by Clyde L. Pilkington, Jr.
Copyright © 2015 by Clyde L. Pilkington, Jr.
All rights reserved.

Original Printing:

  Individual articles published in the *Bible Student's Notebook,*
  2014-2015

Second Printing::
  First book edition, 2015

Executive Editor: André Sneidar
Associate Editors: Richard Lemons; Nadine Sneidar
Layout and Design: Great Adventure in Faith

Cover design by Clyde L. Pilkington, III

      ISBN: 978-1-62904-037-0

Published by

  Bible Student's Press™
  An imprint of *Pilkington & Sons*
  P.O. Box 265
  Windber, PA 15963

For other titles by the author, visit
  www.ClydePilkington.com

For information on *Bible Student's Press*™ releases, visit:
  www.BibleStudentsPress.com

For information on other Bible study resources, visit:
  www.StudyShelf.com

Printed in the United States of America.

CONTENTS

Chapter 1

Introduction

Study to show thyself approved unto God, a workman that needeth not to be ashamed, rightly dividing the Word of Truth (KJV).

Our natural tendency is to view things from the perspective of our own environments. Religious teaching and traditions, along with social norms and standards, play major roles in our preconceived ideas about everything. In other words, it is our predisposition to view everything through religious and social filters.

The believer's journey is a *progressive* freedom from such predetermined notions. An underlying role of the Bible teacher is the challenging of such religious and social viewpoints through the enlightenment of the Scriptures, thus bringing *genuine* liberty to the heart and life of the believer.

The true teacher of Scripture does not exercise dominion over the faith of his listeners but is a helper of their joy, resulting in their individual stand in faith (II Corinthians 1:24).[1] This joyful position in faith is inherent in deliverance from religion's and society's vanity and enslavement (Galatians 5:1).[2]

With this in mind, the goal of this study will be to:

✓ Clarify the truth regarding "study";
✓ Give us greater appreciation for our place on the stage of human history;
✓ Provide gratitude for our access to the Scriptures;
✓ Bring humble thanksgiving to our hearts;
✓ Validate the teaching ministry;
✓ Remind us that modern man should not attach new meaning to Scriptures that did not exist for the contemporaries of its authors;
✓ Remove unnecessary burdens caused by the misuse of Scripture passages.

---

1. "Not that we are lording it over your faith, but are fellow workers of your joy, for you stand fast in the faith" *(Concordant Version)*.
2. "For freedom Christ frees us! Stand firm, then, and be not again enthralled with the yoke of slavery." *(Concordant Version)*.

Chapter 2

An Imaginary "Study"

Imagine with me: You are a student of Scripture. You sit in an empty room. Your purpose in this room is to dedicate yourself to getting to the truth of Scripture. You'll devote the next 10 years to study. Because the room is empty, you'll need to bring your own study resources.

Here are the "rules" for this imaginary "study":

(1) You will not be able to carry your computer or any other electronic devices with you.

(By the way, how many of you came to truth by some electronic means that, only a few years ago, did not even exist? This is extremely humbling, is it not?)

(2) You can bring only 10 books with you.
(3) You will not be able to acquire any additional books once you get there.
(4) Name the 10 books you would bring.

My own personal selections would be:

> *Concordant NT* (1926)
> *Concordant OT* (2008)
> *Concordant Greek Text* (1926)
> *Dabhar Transalation* (2005)
> *The Companion Bible* (Bullinger, 1914)
> *Critical Greek Lexicon* (Bullinger, 1887)
> *Figures of Speech* (Bullinger, 1898)
> *Concordant Commentary* (Knoch, 1968)
> *Strong's Exhaustive Concordance* (1890)
> *The Problem of Evil* (Knoch, 1976)

Notice that I have placed beside each of my selections their original dates of publication. The oldest resource on my list is only 127 years old (1887).[1] (The house I live in is nearly that old!)

What's my point? Well, if I went back to 1886,

---

[1] For historical perspective, 1887 is the year that the US leased Pearl Harbor from Hawaii, and the year that Sir Arthur Conan Doyle's first Sherlock Holmes story was published.

none of my chosen tools would exist. If I wanted them in 1886, I would be forced to re-create all of the eventual work that would end up being done by Bullinger, Knoch, Strong and the various translators of my 10 chosen books.

When we consider how advantaged we are with so many study tools, it is extremely humbling, is it not?

Keep all of this in mind, as we'll revisit this point later.

Chapter 3

Questions Related to "Studying"

Now that we have our imaginary "study" in place, let's ask some basic questions.

Why would anyone study the Scriptures? Would it not be, at least initially, to get at the truth of Scriptures?

Then we must beg to ask, *Exactly what is "studying"?*

Is it simply a matter of reading the Bible? Of reading Bible study books? Of acquiring and utilizing the right Bible study tools?

Is the issue in "Bible Study" the *quality* of effort involved? Is it a matter of applying the right amount of labor? Will the *harder* one studies be a guarantee of anything?

Or, is it an issue of the **quantity** of study? Is it a matter of investing the proper amount of time? Will the *longer* one studies be a guarantee of anything?

Will **any** of these assure that we will acquire knowledge of the truth?

Chapter 4

Is Bible Study the Key to Truth Acquisition?

Take Joel and Tom studying any given topic in Scripture. Let's say Joel spends 30 years studying a certain subject and Tom spends three months studying the same one. Which one will arrive at *the truth* regarding their themes? We can't really answer that question, can we?

The fact that Joel spent 30 years is no guarantee that he will have the correct understanding. The fact that Tom studied for only three months is no indication that his understanding will be incorrect or inadequate.

Let's look at it another way. Let's say Joel has a large library filled with many volumes of Bible study resources, while Tom has only a very meager selection. Now, which one will arrive at *the truth* regarding their themes? Again, we can't answer that question.

The fact that Joel has far greater resource tools is no assurance that he will have the correct understanding, and the fact that Tom has only a handful of aids is no suggestion that his understanding will be incorrect.

That students invests many hours, weeks, months or years in a particular study, and may have amassed large collections of re-source tools, might reveal that they are *passionate* about their subject – but it is no guarantee that they are correct.

Neither does a relatively small amount of time spent in study, with few aids, mean that one is less passionate or that one does not have a firm grasp of the truth.

Paul speaks of those who are,

> *Always learning and yet not at any time able to come into a realization of the truth* (II Timothy 3:7).

Why is this so? How can this be? It is because

the *key* to grasping truth is *faith*, and faith is a *gift.*

> *For by grace are ye saved through faith;*
> *and that not of yourselves: it is the gift of*
> *God* (Ephesians 2:8)

> *For unto you it is given in the behalf of*
> *Christ, not only to believe on Him, but*
> *also to suffer for His sake* (Philippians
> 1:29)

You could even be shut up in your "study" with the Lord Jesus Christ Himself and not get to the truth. We know this because many of those who were exposed to His earthly teaching ministry were blinded to it.

> *Yet, after His having done so many*
> *signs in front of them, they believed*
> *not in Him, that the word of Isaiah*
> *the prophet, which he said, may be be-*
> *ing fulfilled, "Lord, who believes our*
> *tidings? And the arm of the Lord, to*
> *whom was it revealed?" Therefore they*
> *could not believe, seeing that Isaiah*
> *said again that "He has blinded their*
> *eyes and callouses their heart, lest they*

may be perceiving with their eyes, and should be apprehending with their heart, and may be turning about, and I shall be healing them" (John 12:37).

It is important to remember that we don't find God; He finds us. We don't find the truth; the truth finds us.

Truth is not earned or learned – truth is revealed. – Al Stahl

This is extremely humbling, is it not?

Chapter 5

Written to Timothy

This may come as a shock to you, but II Timothy 2:15 is actually *not* an instruction to the Body of Christ at-large, but is a commission to a *certain member* of the Body of Christ: Timothy, Paul's successor.

This instruction, like others found given to Timothy in this same book (*i.e.,* "*Herald the word*"[1] and "*do the work of an evangelist*"[2]) can't properly be charged to the Body of Christ as a whole. Doing so actually violates the rest of injunction to, "*rightly divide the Word of Truth.*"

Please Don't Misunderstand

It is critical that you do not misunderstand my point here. I am not attacking the study

---

1. 4:2.
2. 4:5.

of Scripture, or diminishing its importance in any way. The simple fact is that I have devoted my life to the study of Scripture. It is my passion.

Our main website is *www.StudyShelf.com*, and the slogan at the top of our website says, **"Study** ... *that's what we're all about."*

Our weekly periodical is the *Bible Student's Notebook*. Our main book publishing imprint is *Bible Student's Press*, and our online radio station is *Bible Student's Radio*. So, to think that I am saying that the study of the Scriptures are not important to me would be to misunderstand what I am saying.

Chapter 6

The Underlying Ignorance
Related to "Study"

IGNORANCE OF THE
HISTORY OF LITERACY

Let's first consider literacy[1] in the first century. We'll first hear from a familiar voice. A.E. Knoch speaks to the point of first century literacy when he wrote:

> As few could write, a special class were professional scribes, and, being able to read, they were considered the learned class.[2]

Knoch writes this in the *Concordant Keyword Concordance* regarding *"scribes."* He informs us that men were called *"scribes"* because, in a society when few could read or write, they were a special class who could.

---

1. *The ability to read and write.*
2. *Concordant Keyword Concordance*, scribe, page 259.

Some historians place the literacy rate of the 1st century at less than 10%,[3] while Jewish resources suggest that it was even less than 3%.[4]

RECENT HISTORY OF LITERACY

As for the more recent history of literacy, we will focus on English speaking people.

> Throughout most of history the majority have been illiterate. In feudal society, for example, the ability to read and write was of value only to the clergy and aristocracy. The first known reference to "literate laymen" did not appear until the end of the 14th century. Illiteracy was not seen as a problem until after the invention of printing in the 15th century.[5]

During the 14th century, for example, 80% of English speaking adults could not spell

---

3. "Literacy in the Roman empire, by very rough estimate, did not exceed 10% on average." - Yale Professor Wayne A. Meeks, *The Moral World of the First Christians*, 1986.
4. "Rabbinic sources support evidence that the literacy rate was less than 3%" - M. Bar-Ilan, *Illiteracy in the Land of Israel in the First Centuries C.E.*, S. Fishbane, S. Schoenfeld and A. Goldschlaeger (eds.), *Essays in the Social Scientific Study of Judaism and Jewish Society, II*, New York: Ktav, 1992, pp. 46-61.
5. *The Columbia Encyclopedia.*

their own names.[6] It has not been many generations past that some of our grandfathers wrote an X for their signature.

This is extremely humbling, is it not?

THE PAST 5 CENTURIES OF ENGLISH LITERACY RATES

Look at the chart on page 28 showing the literacy rate of the past few centuries among English speaking peoples.

Notice that, in the middle of the 20th Century, English literacy was almost 95% among English speaking people. At the same time, the literacy rate worldwide was only 56%. So we can see that the issue of literacy was even worse in some groups of people.

FEMALES AND ETHNIC GROUPS

Then think about if we had lived in periods of history where the education of women was diminished as a whole?

Or, what of those periods in American history where it was even illegal to teach slaves

6. *Literacy Rates,* by Tatiana Schlossberg.

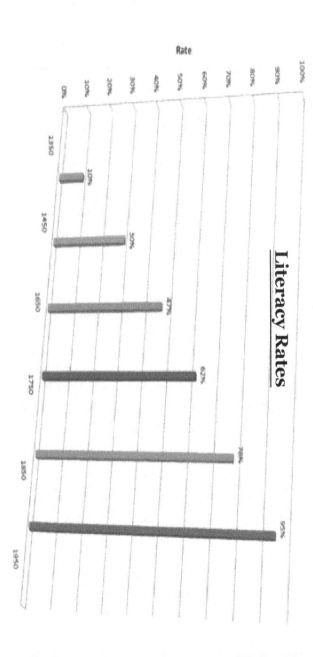

Literacy Rates

Rate

Year	Rate
1350	10%
1450	30%
1690	43%
1750	62%
1850	78%
1950	95%

to read and write?

I am attempting to get us to imagine what it has been like for most of the centuries since Paul and the other writers penned the Greek Scriptures. I am also trying to get us to think of how *extremely* advantaged we are.

SCRIPTURE TRANSLATIONS IN OUR NATIVE TONGUE

Or, suppose we were among the few in history who were literate, but we lived in periods and locations where the Scriptures were not even in our *own* language. Let's say that we were English before the first complete English translation was available in 1384.[7] All we might have access to would have been Greek, Hebrew and Latin. We would have been practically illiterate to the Scriptures, since they would not have been readable to us.

EYESIGHT'S EFFECT ON LITERACY

I am trying to get us to think of all of the obstacles to literacy that we would have faced that

---

7. John Wycliffe is credited for producing the first whole Bible translation into English in 1384. Prior to that there were many portions done.

are not even initially apparent in the statistics. Take fading eyesight for example. Even the literate can't read once their sight has diminished. I wear glasses and can't read my Bible without them. Eyeglasses were invented just in the 13th century, and it took a couple of additional centuries for them to become common.

Even if I were literate in the 12th century, at my current age and eye condition it would not make any practical difference. Or, even if I had lived in subsequent centuries I might not have had *access* to glasses or have been able to *afford* them.

ILLITERACY AND THE IMPORTANCE OF SCRIPTURE

It is important to recognize that illiteracy doesn't suggest that someone is unintelligent; neither does it mean that Scriptures were unimportant. Even with a low literacy rate people could listen to Scripture being read, such as in the synagogue.

*For Moses, from ancient generations, city by city, has those who are heralding him, **being read on every sabbath in the synagogues*** (Acts 15:21).

Scriptures Created a Need for Literacy

Scriptures have often been the actual motivation for literacy. The importance and value of Scripture has had related effects as well, such as the inspiration for the printing press.

Ignorance of the History of Access to the Scriptures

Let's take a quick look at some key points related to the actual access of Scripture through history.

Handwritten Copies

Scriptures had to be handwritten until the invention of the printing press in 1440.

The History of Modern Paper:

The earliest certain evidence of the ancestor of modern paper was with the establishment of the first water-powered paper mill in the 13th century.[8]

---

8. Burns, Robert I. (1996), "Paper comes to the West, 800–1400", in Lindgren, Uta, Europäische Technik im Mittelalter. 800 bis 1400. *Tradition und Innovation* (4th ed.), Berlin: Gebr. Mann Verlag, pp. 417f.

The History of the Modern Pencil:

The "graphite writing implement" was developed in the 16th century[9]

The History of the Modern Pen:

It was Bartholomew Folsch who first received an English patent in 1809 for a pen with an ink reservoir.[10]

How long would it take to write a copy of the entire Bible?

Even with access to hand written copies of Scripture, how long would it take to produce one?

In 2013, Phillip Patterson of New York finished writing out every word in the Bible. Retired, he worked for as many as 14 hours a day on the project, though he averaged around six to eight hours a day.[11]

---

9. Douglas Harper (June 27, 2012) "Pencil," *Online Etymology Dictionary.*
10. Bosworth, C.E. (Autumn 1981), "A Mediaeval Islamic Prototype of the Fountain Pen?" *Journal of Semitic Studies,* XXVI (i),
11. *How long do you think it will take to write the Bible by hand?* Associated Press, Philmont (New York), May 6, 2013.

How many sheets of paper did it take? 2,400.

Patterson had the marked advantage of using modern pens. One source tells us that an ancient scribe might use as many as 80 quills a day.[12]

How easy do you think it was for ancients to obtain paper, ink and quills? If they could have, how much would they have cost?

How many times longer do you think it would take to write the Scriptures by using a quill rather that a modern pen? Laboriously dipping one's quill in the ink well?

How long did it take Peterson with all of his modern conveniences? 4 years.

This is extremely humbling, is it not?

Chapter and Verse Divisions

Even the ease of referencing and locating portions of Scripture is relatively recent. Although these are two-edged swords, creating unnatural breaks that can affect one's understanding of context, I personally could not imagine the study of Scriptures without them. Their value

12. www.biblica.com

in referencing and locating text are immense.

Chapter divisions date back to 1227.[13] Hebrew verse divisions were done in 1448,[14] and the Greek in 1555.[15] In 1560 the *Geneva Bible* was the first English New Testament to have both chapter and verse divisions.

Access to Tools

We set the stage for this point earlier.

Let's just consider the *most basic* of our study tools: *a concordance.*

The first exhaustive English/Hebrew/Greek concordance was published in 1890. It was a culmination of 35 years' work by James Strong[16] and more than 100 of his colleagues.

---

13. By Stephen Langton, professor at the University of Paris and later Archbishop of Canterbury.

14. By Nathan, a Jewish rabbi.

15. By Robert Stephanus, a French printer.

16. Professor of exegetical theology at Drew Theological Seminary.

Chapter 7

Paul Says that Faith Comes by *Hearing* the Tidings of a Herald

So then faith comes by hearing (Romans 10:17).

Consequently, faith is out of tidings, yet the tidings through a declaration of Christ (CV).

This is what Paul twice calls *"the hearing of faith"* (Galatians 3:2, 5). Paul elaborated on this in Romans 10:

How then shall they call on Him in Whom they have not believed? And how shall they believe in Him of Whom they have not heard? And how shall they hear without a herald? And how shall they herald, except they be sent? As it is written, "How beautiful are the feet of them that herald the good news of peace, and bring glad tidings of good things!"

But they have not all obeyed the good
news. For Isaiah said, "Lord, who has
believed our report?" So then faith
comes by hearing, and hearing by the
word of God. But I say, Have they not
heard? Yes certainly, "Their voice went
into all the earth, and their words unto
the ends of the world" (:14-18).

Paul's quotation here (:18) is from Psalm
19:4. Here is the context (:1-4):

The heavens declare the glory of God;
and the firmament shows His handi-
work. Day unto day utters speech, and
night unto night shows knowledge.
There is no speech nor language, where
their voice is not heard. Their voice is
gone out through all the earth, and their
words to the ends of the world.

Creation itself has been the most ancient
revelation and the most heard herald.[1]

---

1. Not to mention the inner awareness of the "testimony of
our conscience" (II Corinthians 1:12) and "premonition"
(Romans 8:19, Concordant Version). "Premonition"
is defined as "intuitive opinion" by the *Concordant*
Keyword Concordance.

Callings Related to the Ministry of the Scriptures

There are many different and diverse parts of Christ's Body. Not all of us have the same calling.

- Some teach. ✓
- Some hear. ✓
- Some verify. ✓

The Order of Romans 10

The divine order as seen in Romans 10 is laid forth as follows:

- Sent ✓
- Spoken ✓
- Heard ✓
- Believed ✓

The Role of the Bible Teacher

God calls and impassions some to (re)search truth and make it public. They are called to check and recheck for confirmation. They seek to unlock truth from tradition, revelation from deception.

The Ethiopian Eunuch

One clearly can notice the role of the herald in Acts 8. The Ethiopian eunuch is reading from the book of Isaiah. Phillip inquired if he understood what he read. His reply was,

How can I except someone guide me?

The Progression of Scripture Teaching

All believers tap into the journey of others: into what they know; what they have studied, read, heard, thought.

Each generation stands on the shoulders of the previous. This is no different for those teaching the Scriptures.

As Otis Q. Sellers has so well written,

> I hope anyone following after me will go further than I have gone in the search for truth, will see more of the Word of God than I have seen, and will explore where I never dreamt treasures were to be found.

What may have taken decades to learn by one student of Scripture (even while standing on the shoulders of others) can be passed on to another in the course of a 30 minute talk or a short article.

What would I know today without the likes of A.E. Knoch, Vladimir Gelesnoff, E.W. Bullinger, A.P. Adams, Andrew Jukes and the innumerable host of those who came before them? Father used them to herald, and graciously granted us the *"hearing of faith."* This is extremely humbling, is it not?

Special Heralds Are Called

We should all be thankful for such men who bring us the Word of God. They are treasures to us. Their feet are beautiful (Romans 10:5).

Their function is not accidental. As Paul and Timothy, they were (II Timothy 2:4):

enlisted (CV);

chosen (KJV);

summoned ... *to serve* (Rotherham).

Their calling is to be heralds and teachers; to stand, *opportunely, inopportunely – exposing, rebuking and entreating, with all patience* (1:11; 4:2).

These heralds find other faithful men entrusting to them that which in turn is to be taught to others – generation upon generation.

> *What things you hear from me through many witnesses, these commit to faithful men, who shall be competent to teach others also* (2:2).

The Basic Ministries of Scripture

Heralds – those who publicly read and proclaim the Scriptures.

κήρυξ (*kērux*)

- a messenger (Thayer)
- PROCLAIMer (Knoch)
- a herald (Bullinger)

I was appointed a herald (I Timothy 2:7).

I was appointed a herald (II Timothy 1:11).

Herald the Word (II Timothy 4:2).

Scribes – those who write (copying Scriptures and writing about Scripture topics).

γραμματεύς (*grammateus*)

One easily can see that this Greek word *grammateus* is where we get our English word "grammar."

- a *writer* (Strong)
- a writer (Bullinger)
- writer (Knoch)

Teachers – those who make the Scriptures clear to the listener

διδάσκαλος (*didaskalos*)

- an *instructor* (Strong)
- an instructor (Bullinger)
- one who instructs (Knoch)

I was appointed ... a teacher of the

nations (I Timothy 2:7).

I was appointed ... a teacher of the nations (II Timothy 1:11).

MY OWN PERSONAL STRUGGLES

There was a period in my life where I had misgivings with such callings – with my own calling – because of my rejection of what I had seen in the false religious division of "clergy" and "laity."

I briefly adopted a viewpoint that allowed no place for the role of teacher: it was an "everyone-a-minister" approach. If there was a meeting, each person was to bring their buckets filled to share and pour out on others.[2]

Others, not knowing or understanding God's present truth, misinterpret and misapply I John 2:27,[3] thus also reaching a false conclusion that there is no place for teachers today.

---

2. A concept influenced by Watchman Nee.
3. "The anointing which you obtained from Him is remaining in you, and you have no need that anyone may be teaching you, but as His anointing is teaching you concerning all, and is true, and is no lie, according as it teaches you also, remain in Him" (*Concordant Version*).

While it is true that all ministry "gifts" and "offices" have ceased, the calling and role of teachers and heralds are divine requirements for today.

The "I-Can't-Help-Its"

I can't help what I do. I've tried to help it; I've tried to quit. I describe what happens to me as, "I have the *I-Can't-Help-Its*."

For those of us called to serve the Body of Christ as teachers, this is extremely humbling.

THE LITERACY OF JESUS CHRIST AND HIS REFERENCES TO READING

Jesus Christ was Literate

Three Scripture passages show that Jesus Christ was literate:

- He knew the letters of the alphabet (John 7:15).

- He could read, as Luke 4:16-30 describes Him reading from the scroll of Isaiah at the synagogue.

- He could write, as John 8:6 tells of Him writing in the dust with his finger.

Jesus Christ Addressed the Subject of Reading *to the Classes Who Were Literate*

Jesus asked the **chief priests, scribes** and **elders,**

Have you not read this Scripture ...? (Mark 11:27; 12:10).

He asked a *Mosaic lawyer,*

What is written in the Law? How do you read? (Luke 10:26).

Jesus asked the **Pharisees,**

Have you never read ...? (Mark 2:24-25).

Have you not read ...? (Matthew 12:2, 5).

He asked the **Sadducees,**

Have you not read ...? (Mark 12:18, 26).

JESUS CHRIST AND PAUL READ THE SCRIPTURES AT THE SYNAGOGUES

Jesus Christ's custom was to read the Scriptures publically at the synagogue.

> *He went to the synagogue, as His custom was, on the Sabbath day. And He stood up to* **read** *... (Luke 4:16).*

Paul had the same custom.

> *Now, after the* **reading** *of the law and the prophets, the chiefs of the synagogue dispatch to them, saying, "Men, brethren, if there is in you any word of entreaty for the people, say it" (Acts 13:15).*

> *Now, traversing Amphipolis and Apollonia, they came to Thessalonica, where there was a synagogue of the Jews. Now, as was Paul's custom, he entered to them, and on three sabbaths he reasons with them from the Scriptures (Acts 17:1-2).*

> *Now the brethren immediately send out both Paul and Silas by night into Berea, who are away, coming along into the*

synagogue of the Jews. Now these were more noble than those in Thessalonica, who receive the Word with all eagerness, examining the Scriptures day by day, to see if these have it thus (Acts 17:10-11).

Now he reasoned in the synagogue on every sabbath and persuaded both Jews and Greeks (Acts 18:4).

Chapter 8

Israels's Holy and Solemn Convocations

The Hebrew Scriptures are filled with examples of the reading of the Law and the Prophets *to* Israel. Whole days were devoted to it.

A great related passage is Nehemiah 8. Here is an abridgment of :1-9

> *All the people were gathered and asked Ezra the scribe to bring the book of the law of Moses. And Ezra brings the law before the assembly, both of men and women. And Ezra the scribe stood on a tower of wood that they made for the purpose. And he opened the book before the eyes of all the people. And when he opened it all the people stood up, and Ezra blessed Yahweh, the great Elohim. And all the*

people bowed. And the law of Elohim was **read** *with explanation – so as to give the meaning, and they gave understanding. And all the people wept at their hearing the words of the law.*

Notice carefully the words of :8, as this is the role of the teacher of Scripture:

So they read in the book in the law of God distinctly, and gave the sense, and caused them to understand the reading (KJV).

+ + + +

Other Examples Cited

He took the book of the covenant, and **read** *in the audience of the people* (Exodus 24:7).

Thou shalt **read** *this law before all Israel in their hearing* (Deuteronomy 31:11).

Afterward he **read** *all the words of the law, the blessings and cursings, according to all that is written in the book of* *the law. There was not a word of all that Moses commanded, which Joshua **read** not before all the congregation of Israel, with the women, and the little ones, and the strangers that were conversant among them* (Joshua 8:34).

*Shaphan the scribe shewed the king, saying, "Hilkiah the priest hath delivered me a book." And Shaphan **read** it before the king* (II Kings 22:10).

The king went up into the house of the LORD, *and all the men of Judah and all the inhabitants of Jerusalem with him, and the priests, and the prophets, and all the people, both small and great: and he **read** in their ears all the words of the book of the covenant which was found in the house of the* LORD (II Kings 23:2).

*Therefore go thou, and **read** in the roll, which thou hast written from my mouth, the words of the* LORD *in the ears of the people in the* LORD's *house upon the fasting day: and also thou shalt **read** them in the ears of all Judah that come out of their cities … Then **read** Baruch in the book the words* *of Jeremiah in the house of the* LORD, *in the chamber of Gemariah the son of Shaphan the scribe, in the higher court, at the entry of the new gate of the* LORD's *house, in the ears of all the people* (Jeremiah 36:6, 10).

Chapter 9

Paul's Instructions Regarding Reading

Paul has three instructions in his epistles related to reading.

Two refer to his letters being read *to* the saints.

> *Whenever the epistle should be **read to you,** cause that it should be read in the Laodicean ecclesia also, and that you also may be reading that out of Laodicea* (Colossians 4:16).

> *I am adjuring you by the Lord, that this epistle be **read to all** the holy brethren* (I Thessalonians 5:27).

One refers to Timothy reading.

> *Till I come, give heed to **reading**, to en-*
> *treaty, to teaching (I Timothy 4:13).*

Here is the *only* instruction in Paul's letters
for an individual to read. Even this one is not
so much for Timothy to be reading *for him-*
self, but *to others.*

We know this because the remaining two
things to which he is to give heed in the passage are *entreaty* and *teaching* – both things
that he would not do *to himself,* but *to others.*
So, even this instruction is for the Scriptures
to be read *to others.*

Beyond Academics

Ours is a call to go beyond merely academics.
Studying the Scriptures is not our goal; it is the
means to our goal. Our goal is to know Him.[1]

---

1. *"Him"* is a reference to Christ Jesus, Who is the *"Image"*
    of His Father (Colossians 1:15), Whose [Christ] very
    purpose is to unfold Him [God] (*"He **unfolds** Him,"*
    John 1:18, *Concordant Version*). To know more about
    the Father, one must know more about the work and
    ministry of His Son (*"He who has seen Me has seen the*
    Father," John 14:9; *"neither knows any man the Father,*
    save the Son, and he to whomsoever the Son will re-
    veal Him," Matthew 11:27). For more information on this

Paul's passion went beyond simply the academic: he desired to *"know Him"* (Philippians 3:10). His unceasing prayer for the believer was that God would give them a *"spirit of wisdom and revelation in the realization of Him"* (Ephesians 1:17), that they would *"walk worthily of the Lord for all pleasing, bearing fruit in every good work, and growing in the realization of God"* (Colossians 1:10), and that their love would super-abound in realization (Philippians 1:9).

theme see, "ONE LAYER AT A TIME:The Unfolding of God," by Clyde L. Pilkington, Jr. (*Bible Student's Notebook* #423).

Chapter 10

Long-Standing Assumptions

In addition to the misuse of II Timothy 2:15 there are also other long-standing assumptions that have been used to abuse members of Christ's Body. We will consider a few of them.

Scripture Quotation

Many assume that it is always necessary to fill our conversations with Scripture quotations along with the citing of their books, chapters and verses.

Consider Joel and Tom mentioned earlier. Suppose that Joel shares some things with a friend and fills it with Scripture quotations and references. On the other hand Tom shares some things with little or no such quotations and references. Are we to assume that Joel is sharing truth and conversely Tom is not? Of course not.

Acts 17:22-31 records Paul's message to the pagan Athenians on Mars' Hill. It is important to note the conspicuously complete absence of any use of Scripture by him – not even once. Perhaps just as interesting, the only quotation by Paul is one of a heathen poet.

What is so striking about this is that we are often taught that the God-honoring method of communicating with the lost (*i.e.,* "witnessing," "soul winning," "preaching," etc.) is to riddle our "messages" with Scripture references. In some circles, one's spirituality may even be judged based on the amount of Scripture memorized and delivered during such an "evangelistic" opportunity.

Really, think about it: can you even imagine Paul addressing lost pagans and never even reciting a passage from Scripture? If we had such an opportunity ourselves, many of us would surely believe that we were unfaithful and negligent if we "failed" to use as much of the Bible as we possibly could.

Not that sharing the Scriptures is never to be done with the lost, for surely Paul did; but maybe we should learn a little something from Paul here, and not make our conversations with the lost such a *rote and quote* of Scripture. Maybe, like Paul, we simply should seek to find a place of identification with them – in something that they know and understand – something that is in their frame of reference – something that is important to them; just as he did with their idol to the *"Unknown God,"* and their heathen poetry.

Maybe we should learn to talk to our "Athenians" about sports, movies and other cultural and social interests that they may have, and in these things interpret a divine meaning in life, just as Paul did with the people in his day.

SCRIPTURE MEMORIZATION

Some people have been gifted with amazing memories. I have a cousin who seems to remember nearly every fact he reads or hears. Trust me, you want this man on your team if you are doing trivia night.

Let's say that Joel is so gifted and has memorized much of the Bible – being able to recite it word for word with its location. Tom, on the other hand, struggles with his memory, and only after much effort does he know even a few passages and where to find them.

Which has a greater grasp of truth? Joel, or Tom? Which one loves God and His Word more? Can this be measured by memorization alone? No.

Surely the memorization of Scripture is a worthy thing, but we need to be careful not to make mandates where *God Himself* hasn't.

One Bible passage is used to insist that Scripture memorization be done:

> *Your Word have I hidden in my heart, that I might not sin against You* (Psalm 119:11).

The first thing we note in this verse is the lack of any mandate. This is not a *commandment,* but merely a personal *confession* of the Psalmist.

Second, a closer look shows that there is *no* reference to rote memorization either. It is mere assumption that hiding God's Word in one's heart can be accomplished only by memorization.

Rotherham's translation brings to bear the meaning of the passage:

> *In my heart, have I treasured what Thou hast said, to the end I may not sin against Thee.*

Herein lies the true issue: a treasuring of God's Word – a valuing of His Truth. Some may indeed express this through memorization.

"The Walking Bible"

When I was young an evangelist came through our town, holding a city-wide "crusade." His name was Jack Van Impe. He is known as "The Walking Bible." In fact, he had a biography with that title. It's a reference to the amount of Scripture he has memorized. According to his website, he has spent about

35,000 hours memorizing 14,000 verses.[1]

What, if any, conclusion can we make? Does this mean that he has more truth than other teachers? That he loves, and is more faithful to, God and His Word? That he sins less? – *"that I might not sin against Thee."*

BEING A BEREAN

The brethren immediately sent away Paul and Silas by night to Berea: who coming there went into the synagogue of the Jews. These were more noble than those in Thessalonica, in that they received the Word with all readiness of mind, and searched the Scriptures daily, whether those things were so. Therefore many of them believed; also of honorable women which were Greeks, and of men, not a few (Acts 17:10-12).

I used to cite this passage regularly as a companion to II Timothy 2:15. The constant appeal was to "Be a Berean!" The concept is so popular that I have known organizations and periodicals that even

1. For a frame of reference, the "New Testament" has some 7,956 verses.

have used "Berean" proudly as a part of their name.[2]

Now, as I think of it, if it was not so serious a misuse, it would almost be amusing. Reading the passage carefully, let us note a few things that may get overlooked:

- There is *no instruction* anywhere in this passage to "Be a Berean";
- There is *no instruction* anywhere in this passage to "Search the Scriptures";
- There is *no instruction* anywhere in this passage to "Study";
- This is an account of what happened in a *Jewish synagogue*;
- Those who searched the Scriptures were *unbelievers.*

As was his custom, Paul went to the Jewish synagogue when he arrived at the town of Berea. This was not only the divine principle – *"to the Jew first"* – that was central to his Acts ministry, but had the added benefit of being the ideal place to begin his teaching. After all, the synagogue in Berea was the

---

2. *Berean Bible Society, Berean Searchlight, Berean Publishing Trust, Berean Expositor, Berean Bible Church, Berean Ministries, Berean Advocate, etc.*

sure place to find the Hebrew Scriptures and those who could read them.

When in a new city Paul's first stop was to see those who had possession of, and could read the Scriptures. Not only that, but the Jewish leaders were there; it was the place of their *vocation*. This is why, when Paul read to and taught them from the Scriptures, they had both the time and ability to *"search the Scriptures daily, whether those things were so."* After all, they *could read* and it was their *job*.

The Jewish leaders at Berea's synagogue *"were more noble"* than the leaders at Thessalonica's synagogue, because they actually *"received the Word with all readiness of mind, and searched the Scriptures daily, whether those things were so."* As a result, many of them (and accompanying Jew and Gentile proselytes) believed.

The fact remains, however, that searching the Scriptures is indeed a very noble thing, but not a burden of command to be laid on the back of those who lack God-given ability or passion.

READING THROUGH
THE BIBLE IN A YEAR

There is a popular regimen in certain parts of Christendom: reading through the Bible in a year. They even have special guides and Bibles to assist you in the task. It is a yearly exercise with which many are burdened. Some religious organizations will issue a "certificate" for those professing accomplishment of such a task. How is that working out for them? Are folks coming to the truth? Do they have the (*"hearing of faith"*?)Are they growing in the realization of Him? Not necessarily.

There is nothing wrong with reading the Bible, and if one is so personally motivated to read "from cover to cover" through all of the history of Israel's kings and their long lists of genealogies – it no doubt *could* be a good thing. Yet to burden others with a duty not commissioned to them by God is a disservice to and an abuse of the members of Christ's Body.

Chapter 11

Conclusions

Our desire has been to clarify the truth regarding "Bible study," as well as to provide a greater appreciation for our place on the stage of human history, thus giving us a sense of grateful indebtedness for our access to the Scriptures and the tools in which to study them.

We also trust that this will bring about humble thanksgiving as well as validation of the teaching ministry, while removing the unnecessary burden placed on many by the misuse of Scripture passages.

Finally, we are reminded that passages of Scripture *never* should have meaning to the modern man that they did not to the contemporary of its authors.

Your Part

Now that you have read this book, it's your turn.

If the truths presented here have helped you, don't let these truths die in your hands.

Please write to us and let us know your thoughts concerning its content.

Consider assisting us in getting this book into the hands of those who would be encouraged and strengthened by its message:

- Recommend it to your friends and loved ones.

- Order additional copies to give as gifts.

- Keep extra copies on hand to loan to others.

If you have not read the author's other works, order them today.

We would be honored to have your fellowship in getting this book freely to those who hunger spiritually. We have daily opportunities to send it to pastors, Sunday school teachers, Bible college professors and students, Bible class teachers, and prisoners.

Do You Subscribe to the
Bible Student's Notebook™ *?*

This is a periodical that ...

- Promotes the study of the Bible.
- Encourages the growth of the believer in grace.
- Supports the role of the family patriarch.

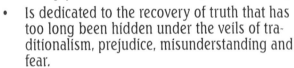

- Is dedicated to the recovery of truth that has too long been hidden under the veils of traditionalism, prejudice, misunderstanding and fear.
- Is not connected with any "Movement," "Organization," "Mission," or separate body of believers, but is sent forth to and for all saints.

The *Bible Student's Notebook*™ is a *free* electronic publication published weekly (52 times a year).

SUBSCRIBE TODAY!

To receive your *free* electronic subscription, email us at:
bsn@studyshelf.com

By *special order* you may also subscribe to a printed, mailed edition for only $1.00 per issue (to cover production and mailing costs). Example: ½ Year (26 issues) = $26; 1 Year (52 issues) = $52

Bible Student's Notebook™
PO Box 265 Windber, PA 15963
www.BibleStudentsNotebook.com
1-800-784-6010

DAILY EMAIL GOODIES™

Do you receive our
Daily Email Goodies™?

These are free daily emails that contain short quotes, articles, and studies on Biblical themes.

These are the original writings of Clyde L. Pilkington, Jr, as well as gleanings from other authors.

<u>Here is what our readers are saying:</u>

"Profound! Comforting! Calming! Wonderful!" – NC

"The Daily Email Goodies continue to bless my heart! ... They provide plenty of food for thought." – IL

"I really appreciate the Goodies!" – VA

"Your Daily Email Goodies are making me aware of authors whose names I don't even know." – GA

"I am glad to be getting the Daily Email Goodies – keep 'em coming." – IN

Request to be added to our free
Daily Email Goodies™

If you would like to be added to the mailing list, email us at:
Goodies@StudyShelf.com

Believer's Warfare, The: Wearing the Armor of Light in the Darkness of this World

(#7000) The believer is in the middle of an ancient spiritual warfare that is as old as mankind. The battle itself, although intense, is not complicated. It is not a process of spiritual hoop-jumping. Indeed it is simple. The Believer's Warfare surveys a few key passages of Scripture to reveal God's sure plan of victory in the life of His saints. – 48 pp., BK.

Bible Student's Notebook, The (VOLUMES)

The Bible Student's Notebook is a periodical dedicated to the: - Promotion of Bible study - Encouragement of the believer's growth in grace - Support of the role of family patriarch - Recovery of truth that has too long been hidden under the veils of traditionalism, prejudice, misunderstanding and fear. The Bible Student's Notebook is not connected with any "Church," "Movement," "Organization," "Society," "Mission," or separate body of believers, but is sent forth to and for all of God's saints. Available in Paperback Volumes.

I Choose! Living Life to Its Fullest

(#4120) Forty-Eight Daily Thoughts on Divine Life. You are alive! Yet not just alive, but alive with the very life of God! Don't allow your "What if ..." imaginations of the past or the future to lay claim to the present that God has given you. Allow the objective, unchanging truth of who God has made you in the Lord Jesus Christ to transform your mind and life as you take this spiritual journey of "I Choose." – 192 pp., PB.

Church in Ruins, The: Brief Thoughts on II Timothy

(#3325) This brief survey of Paul's last epistle will reveal that, while almost 2000 years have transpired, the condition of the church has remained the same, and indeed has worsened in accordance with Paul's warning to Timothy. This book is not a call for a re-awakening of "the church," because it is apparent that this is not Father's plan. Rather, it is a call to individual men – men whose place in the Christian religious system has left them empty, stagnant and restless – to awaken to Father's call to be His faithful servant and stand outside of that system to look for other faithful men as well. – 128 pp., PB.

Daily Goodies: 365 Thoughts on Scriptural Truths

(#1747) This is a great resource for personal and family study, as well as a valuable reference volume covering many varied biblical themes. This is a collection of choice selections from the author's Daily E-mail Goodies. These free daily e-mails began being issued in 2003 and contain studies on scriptural themes. – 490 pp., PB.

Daily Gleanings – 365 Selections on Scriptural Truths

(#1836) This book contains a collection of gleanings from some 200 different authors. These excerpts are intended to be an encouragement to those who are walking on a different path with the Lord – a journey that is *"outside of the camp."*

Some quotations are from beloved and trusted authors, but more often than not, they are from unusual sources. Sometimes, it is simply amazing how an author can admit in print to some grand truth that their writings and ministries otherwise generally deny. For the authors of these quotes, the truth that is conveyed by them may oddly seem "out of place"; but in some ways, the more unlikely the source, the more amazingly it testifies to the truth – and the fact that it cannot be hidden. – 253 pp., PB.

Due Benevolence: A Study of Biblical Sexuality

(#3775) Think you have read all that there is on the subject of sexuality from the Bible? Think again! Religious moralists have taken the wonderful gifts of human beauty and sexuality, and made them something dirty and sinful. Much is at stake regarding truth, as well as the nature and character of God Himself. A groundbreaking work providing:

- A refreshingly honest and uninhibited look at sexuality.
- A breath of fresh air from the religious and Victorian mentality.
- A daring and valuable glimpse at the wonderful light just outside sexuality's prison-cell door.

– 220 pp., PB.

God's Holy Nation: Israel and Her Earthly Purpose (Contrasted with the Body of Christ and Its Heavenly Purpose)

(#2275) Israel plays a key role in God's plan of the ages. Though currently she has been set aside "until the times of the nations be fulfilled," He is by no means done with her.

Today, God is operating His purpose in the ecclesia – the Church, the Body of Christ. The Scriptures provide us with the clear, critical distinction between God's earthly nation and Christ's celestial body.

Christendom, however, has diminished Israel's divine significance in an attempt to advance their artificial homogenization of Scripture's grand theme, thus obscuring the glorious evangel of our day – "the Good News of the Happy God" committed to the trust of Paul, our Apostle.

This work highlights some of the more prominent distinctions which belong to God's literal, physical, earthly nation. In so doing, it is our desire to allow the reader to see more clearly God's dealings with God's favored nation, so that they may in turn embrace a far greater calling and purpose. – 360 pp., PB.

Heaven's Embassy: The Divine Plan & Purpose of the Home

(#5675) The home is central to all of God's dealings with man throughout the course of time. It is His Divine "institution" and "organization" upon the earth, and for the believer, it is the Embassy of Heaven. An embassy is "the residence or office of an ambassador." Since the believer is an ambassador of the Lord Jesus Christ (II Corinthians 5:14-21), his home is thus the Divine Embassy of heavenly ministry. Pauline ministry is centered in the homes of believers. This is even the true sphere of the Body of Christ; for this reason our apostle speaks of "church in thy house." This book doesn't focus upon the external specifics of the ministry of Heaven's Embassy (such as hospitality); that will be saved for another volume. Instead, it looks at the inner-workings of the Embassy itself; focusing upon its very nature and internal purpose and function. – 250 pp., PB.

I Am! Who and What God Says I Am! The Divine Reckoning of the Renewed Mind; Daily Thoughts on Divine Life

(#1737) People are always talking about their attempts to discover their true selves – of trying to "find themselves." The believer in the Lord Jesus Christ needs to find out who they *really* are. This doesn't need to be such a difficult search. All that is really needed is a careful look at the Scriptures, and a simple faith in the words of who and what God says we are. God knows who we are; all we need

to do is to *believe Him.* This book catalogs the Divine Record of who and what God says that you are. It is a short encyclopedia of faith – the truth about you. It is the truth about you, simply because it is *God* Who has said it. God has spoken these truths concerning you – the *real* you. Believe His record! Refuse to be the shell of a person, pushed into a mold of Adamic conformity. Be the real you that God has uniquely designed you to be. Refuse to be bullied out of your divinely designed identity that our Father has given you. – 107 pp., PB.

Outsiders, The: God's Called-Out Ones – A Biblical Look at the Church – God's Ecclesia

(#4125) In 1995, after sixteen years of being in the "pastorate" the author walked away. He left the "religious system" by resigning from the very "church" and "ministry" he had formed. In many ways this work is a testament to these actions. This testimony was thirty years in the making – the results of a spiritual journey that the author found to be common to other saints scattered throughout the world and across history. This is an opportunity to explain why some who love the Lord no longer "go to church." It does not seek to persuade others to do something different; but rather to be simply who and what they already are "in Him." This is an uncovering of the truth of the church, and an encouragement for the members of His Body to enjoy the position and standing "in Christ" that they already possess, realizing that they are truly *"complete in Him"* (Colossians 2:10), that He alone is their Life (Colossians 3:4), and that His Life is full of freedom (Galatians 5:1). – 128 pp., PB.

World Affairs and National Politics – and the High Calling of God in Christ Jesus

(#4250) When did nationalism begin? What is God's purpose for nationalism? Is the United States a Christian nation? Does any government have Favored Nation Status with God today? Should believers support Israel? What did Paul have to say about our citizenship? What is our role in relation to nations? Is our job to rid the world of evil? What should the believer's attitude be toward earthly authority? Should all obedience to earthly magistrates be absolute? Are believers to pay their taxes? Where does voting and jury duty fit in? Why was the apostle Paul executed? These and many other questions are addressed in this groundbreaking work! – 258 pp., PB.

Suffering: God's Forgotten Gift

Two gifts given to the believer are mentioned by Paul in Philippians 1:29. The first is *"to believe on Him."* This is a glorious gift. Every believer has been given this gift from God. Those who possess it may not even fully recognize it as a gift from Him, but indeed faith is God's wonderful gift to us. Faith is a rich gift from God, but there is also another gift from God to the believer mentioned by Paul in Philippians 1:29 that is equally as glorious. The second gift is *"also to suffer for His sake."* This, too, is a glorious gift. Every believer has been given this gift from God as well, but those who possess it often do not fully recognize it for what it is. Indeed, suffering for His sake similarly is God's wonderful gift to us. Paul teaches us to embrace this second gift as well as we do the first! – 100 pp., PB.

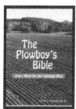

Plowboy's Bible, The: God's Word for Common Man

(#4425) Shocking conclusions from the man that brought you The King James Bible Song. This book represents years of study and a significant change in understanding. Raised on and trained in a "King James Only" position, most of the author's teaching ministry was centered on the defense of the KJV. He had early associations with major proponents of this position and their followers. He actively taught classes and seminars on the subject of Bible versions. For many years he distributed thousands of books from a collection of over 100 different titles in support of the KJV position. Here he shares what he has come to see that has caused him to completely abandon his former position. – 254 pp., PB.

Salvation Of ALL, The: Creation's Final Destination (A Biblical Look at Universal Reconciliation)

(#7001) The Gospel of our Lord and Savior, Jesus Christ is truly better "Good News" than we could ever have imagined. It is far more glorious than religion would ever have us believe. The Salvation of All is a book about a "Good News" that will reach its final goal in the salvation of all mankind. – 302 pp., PB.

Being OK with Not Being OK: Embracing God's Design for You – and Everyone You Know (and Don't Know)

(#1985) For now, you're broken, and you aren't going to be "fixed." Granted, you may have some days that are better than others, some circumstances that seem to indicate that you are "OK," but the wearisome cycle simply will recur.

Thus it is by design – by divine design. Father is bringing you to a place where you are OK with not being OK, where you simply rest in His current purpose and plan in your training and development for that grand and magnificent culmination that He has so wonderfully and skillfully designed especially for you – in your next life. – 134 pp., PB.

King James Version, The – 400 Years of Bondage – 1611-2011

(#4682) 1611 was not a high spiritual mark in the history of the church, the Body of Christ. Instead of being a grand year of the pinnacle of preservation or perfection of God's Word, it was rather the sad depths of the subtle corrupting of God's Word by the historic union of governmental and ecclesiastical politics. – 72 pp., PB.

Nothing Will Be Lost! The Truth About God's Good News

(#3750) This is an abridgement of the larger work The Salvation of All. It is designed as a give-away edition, with quantity pricing available. – 88 pp., PB.

Steps I Have Taken, The – *A Short Autobiographical Work*

(#1175) Many times over the years Clyde has been asked how he got from an Independent Baptist pastor to where he is now: from a hell-fire and brimstone street preacher to a herald of the good news of "the happy God." This work is a short chronicle of his journey: leaving the confines of religious bondage to enjoying the life of God in the wide open spaces of His grace. – 65 pp., PB.

Myth of Easter, The – *"The Christian Mythology"* Series

(#1675) There are many myths in Christendom that have managed to master their own form of mythology. Easter is an example of such a religious fable. If Easter is the celebration of the historical fact of our Lord Jesus Christ's resurrection, then why does its date change every year? It is one of the glaring clues that something is seriously wrong with Christendom. Have you ever really considered if there is any scriptural basis of Good Friday or Easter Sunrise Services, or what Easter Rabbits and Easter Eggs have to do with the resurrection of Christ or teachings of God's Word? Although millions of people are of the opinion that Easter and all of its customs are Christian and originated as a result of Christ's resurrection, it is a historical fact that the observance of Easter long antedates Christianity by centuries. – 31 pp., BK.

Enjoy Books?

Visit us at:

www.StudyShelf.com

Over the years we have often been asked to recommend books. The requests come from believers who longed for material with substance. Study Shelf™ is a collection of books which are, in our opinion, the very best in print. Many of these books are "unknown" to the members of the Body of Christ at large, and most are not available at your local "Christian" bookstore.

YOU CAN:

Read

A wealth of articles from past issues of the *Bible Student's Notebook*™

Purchase

Rare and hard to find books, booklets, leaflets, Bibles, etc. in our 24/7 online store.